Select and Clean Shells

Only collect shells that have washed up on the beach.
Select different sizes and colors of unbroken shells.
Or you can purchase whole, drilled, or cut shells.
Note: Shells still in the water may contain a living animal.

1. Scrape away barnacles and lime buildup with a sharp knife.
2. Wipe away surface sand and dirt with a damp cloth, rubbing hard on stubborn spots.

3. Whiten discolored sanddollars and shells by soaking in a solution of 1 part chlorine bleach to 4 parts water.
4. To clean openings in small shells, pry out sand and dirt with a nut pick and wipe clean with a cotton swab.

5. Remove stubborn buildup by soaking in Lime remover then scraping. Some shells require a month of soaking and scraping, but can be cleaned with patience and elbow grease.
6. Dry wet shells thoroughly, up to several hours for soaked shells. Use a fan or hairdryer for larger shells.
   Note: Glue will not stick to damp shells.

Design Construction

Twist and turn shells to find the best fit and prettiest side. Build shell designs from the bottom up. Put glue on the bottom of a top shell and place it on top of other shells. The glue will run down onto the shell below and bond.

To put small shells into tight spaces, glue a shell to the tip of a stick with a tiny drop of glue. Cool. Apply glue to the bottom of the shell, insert into desired space with the stick, press down until cool, twist the stick and remove it.

To remove or reposition shells, melt glue with point of a hot glue gun, holding in place until glue reheats and shell becomes loose. Heat resistant designs can be carefully heated in oven, with a heat gun or hair dryer. Caution! Shells will be very hot!

Finishing

Use non-yellowing Clear acrylic spray to coat the shells.
Use Clear acrylic ultra fine glitter. Apply while spray is tacky.

Mini Angel Pins
by Nancy Flodine

SIZE: 2" x 2"
SHELLS:
   1½" Pecten or Clam shell for skirt
   Two ¾" Kitten's Paw shells for wings
   Two ½" Dove shells for arms
MATERIALS:
   1 White 6 mm pearl, 1" pin back
   Metallic Gold acrylic paint
   Clear acrylic spray, Hot glue
   Extra fine Clear acrylic glitter
INSTRUCTIONS:
   If necessary, cut "wings" off skirt shell with side cutters. Glue Paw shell wings to Pecten or Clam shell skirt. Glue Dove shell arms, open sides down, into indent between wings and skirt.

   Lightly brush Gold paint on edges of shells and across textured areas to highlight. Paint solid Gold edge around skirt bottom. Spray, sprinkle with glitter while tacky. Glue pearl in place.

   Let cool. Reinforce angel with extra glue on back, filling wings and all open spaces. Dry flat. Glue pin to back.

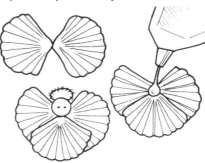

Smile

by Andrea Gibson

SIZE: 4" x 5"
SHELLS: Assorted shells
MATERIALS:
 Decorative papers, 6 Lime brads
 Sakura Black ink pens (.05)
 Wiggle eyes, Blue flower
INSTRUCTIONS:
 Cut decorative paper 4" x 10½". From one end, fold at ½" and 5½". Fold into a matchbook shape. Cut a Green mat 3⅜" x 4¼". Ink the edges. Adhere to card. Position shells to form pig. Trace around the shells, drawing a pig shape. Glue shells and wiggle eyes in place. Write "you make me" at the top.
 Write the letters for "SMILE" on White paper. Cut out, adhere to card. Attach brads. Fold matchbook. Secure bottom fold with Blue flower and brad.

Top Dog

by Andrea Gibson

SIZE: 5" x 6"
SHELLS: Assorted shells
MATERIALS:
 Cardstock (Brown, Red, White)
 Rub-on letters, Hot glue
 Sakura Black ink pen (.05)
 Rubber Stamping Ink (Red, Black, Brown)
 Wiggle eyes, Silver brad, Brown ⅛" wide ribbon
INSTRUCTIONS:
 Make a Brown card 5" x 6". Cut a Red mat 4¼" x 5½". Cut a White mat 4" x 5⅛". Ink the edges. Adhere mats to card. Rub on "Top dog".
 Arrange shells in a dog shape. Position ribbon as a collar and brad as a dog tag. Glue in place. Adhere wiggle eyes. Draw around dog with a pen.

Welcome

by Andrea Gibson
SIZE: 4¼" x 5½"
SHELLS: Assorted shells
MATERIALS:
 Cardstock (Green, White)
 Decorative papers
 Sakura Black pen (.05)
 Chalk inks (Green, Brown), Wiggle eyes
 Red ⅛" wide ribbon, White tag, Dragonfly brad
INSTRUCTIONS:
 Fold a White card to 4¼" x 5½". Cut a decorative paper mat 4" x 5¼". Cut a Green mat 3¼" x 4⅞". Ink edges. Adhere mats to card.
 Position shells to form a frog shape. Glue shells and wiggle eyes in place. Draw around the shape with a pen. Ink the edges of the tag. Tie ribbon through tag. Write message. Attach brad. Adhere tag to corner of card.

Seashell Shadowbox
by Cyndi Hansen

SIZE: 10" x 10"
SHELLS: Assorted shells
MATERIALS:
    Shadowbox 10" x 10"
    Decorative papers
    Cosmo Cricket (Border stickers, Chipboard letters)
    Black foam core board
    White stamp pad and embossing powder
    Deckle edge scissors
    Heat gun, Craft glue, Pop dots, Large glue dots
INSTRUCTIONS:
    Measure inside of box and cut foam core pieces following the diagram. Cut notches so the pieces fit together. Place inside of box to verify the fit. Remove foam core, cut background papers and adhere to back of foam core. Let dry. Adhere this piece to backboard.
    Cover edges of foam core with sticker borders.
    Print quote on cardstock and cut out with deckle edge scissors. Stamp the front of each letter with ink and sprinkle with embossing powder. Heat set.
    Adhere shells, starfish, letters, and quote in place.
    Assemble frame and adhere borders to front of box.

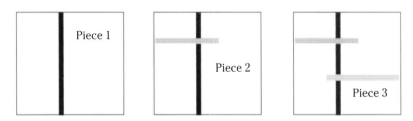

Shadowbox - Foam core pieces front view diagram

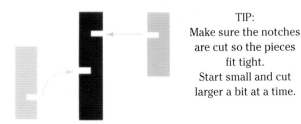

Shadowbox - Foam core pieces side view with notches.

TIP:
Make sure the notches are cut so the pieces fit tight.
Start small and cut larger a bit at a time.

Snowflake Ornament
by Linda Valentino
Size: 4" x 4"
SHELLS:
   18 Cockle shells, Jingle shell for center
MATERIALS:
   4" wooden snowflake, White acrylic paint
   Fine iridescent glitter, Silver cord
   Clear 7mm rhinestone
INSTRUCTIONS:
Paint snowflake and shells with White. Sprinkle glitter over snowflake while wet. Let dry. Adhere shells. Glue rhinestone on Jingle shell in center. Add Silver cord as hanger.

Angel in a Frame
by Julie McGuffee
SIZE: 4" x 6"
SHELLS:
   1 small Sand Dollar for halo
   Baby Ark shells (2 for wings, 2 small for arms)
   2 small Pearlized Snail shells for feet
   1 White Pecten for dress
MATERIALS:
   Frame with 4" x 6" opening, 4" x 6" Pink matboard
   18"of Off White-Gold ⅝" wide wire edged ribbon
   9" of Off White ½" wide ruffled lace

18" Off White 4mm pearls by the yard
Dried Baby's Breath, Mauve silk rose
Gold ring, ¾" wood button plug
Sphagnum moss, 3 Pink ¼" roses
INSTRUCTIONS:
Remove glass from frame. Glue lace to inside bottom and top edges of frame. Glue mat in opening. Adhere shells, referring to photo. Glue wood plug in center for head. Glue moss on head and shells for arms on front of dress. Glue pearls along indentations in dress shell, around neck and around top edge of Sand Dollar. Glue roses on front of dress and ring on head. Glue on feet. Tie ribbon bow and glue in place. Glue small sprigs of Baby's Breath and silk rose to center of bow.

Cross
by Andrea Gibson
SIZE: 3" x 5"
SHELLS:
   Assorted small to medium
MATERIALS:
   Paper mache or wooden cross
   White craft paint, Tacky glue
INSTRUCTIONS:
Paint cross. Let dry. Glue shells onto cross.

Shell Doll Ornament
by Julie McGuffee
SIZE: 3" x 3¾"
SHELLS:
   2 White Scallop shells, 1 Trochus
   1 tiny Trochus, 1 small Snail
MATERIALS:
   ¾" wood ball, Jute
   ⅛" diameter dowel stick
   18" Blue ⅛" wide ribbon
   4" White 3mm pearls by the yard
INSTRUCTIONS:
Body: Glue Scallops together back to back. Glue wood ball on top.
Hair: Wrap jute around a stick. Hold in place and lay a thin bead of glue along jute. Let dry.
   Remove jute. Glue Trochus to top of head. Glue hair around shell. Glue pearls around top of hair.
Necklace: Glue pearls around neck with a tiny Trochus in front.
Hanger: Thread 8" of ribbon through the space between the scallop shells. Tie the ends together. Make a bow with the remaining ribbon and glue to top of hanger. Glue Snail shell to center of bow.

Shell Flowers Frame

Shells form delicate flowers in a beautiful frame.

by Julie McGuffee

SIZE: 6½" x 8½"

SHELLS:
Assorted Apple Blossom and Coquina shells for petals
Dentalium for butterfly
Small Snail shells

MATERIALS:
Wood frame with a 5" x 7" opening
5" x 7" Green matboard
3" round White crocheted doily
26" Off White 4mm pearls by the yard
1 yard of White-Gold ⅛" wide ribbon
Wax paper, Glue gun

INSTRUCTIONS:

FRAME AND MAT:
Place matboard in frame. Glue ribbon border on mat. Glue pearls on frame.

DOILY BASKET:
Fold edges of doily up. Glue in place on the mat. Tie a bow with ribbon. Glue to doily.

PANSIES:
Make 2. Place 2 Coquina shells and 1 Apple Blossom face down on wax paper. Glue together. Let dry. Turn shells over. Place a small dab of glue where shells join. Place 2 smaller Coquina shells into glue. Let dry. Glue small pearl to center.

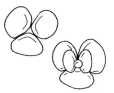

ROSES:
Make 2 large and 1 small. Place a dab of glue on wax paper. Working quickly, gently press 5 Apple Blossom shells in glue at a slight angle. Let dry. Place more glue in center and press 4 more shells in glue. Let dry. Gently remove from wax paper. Glue pearl in center. Make small rose with 3 outer and 3 inner shells, glue pearl in center.

STAR FLOWER:
Make 1. Place 5 Coquina shells face down on wax paper. Glue in center. Let dry. Remove from wax paper. Glue a small Snail shell in center.

3-PETAL FLOWER:
Make 2. Place 3 Coquina shells face down on wax paper. Glue in center. Let dry. Remove from wax paper. Glue a pearl in the center.

FINISH FLOWERS:
Glue flowers to mat.

BUTTERFLY:
Glue 2 small Coquina shells to a Dentalium shell then glue the butterfly to mat.

Sailor's Love Knot

Express your heartfelt love for the sea.

SIZE: 6½" x 8½"

SHELLS: 6 Baby Ark shells, 6 Turitella shells

MATERIALS:
28" of sisal rope
36" Seafoam Green satin ½" wide ribbon
36" White 4mm pearls by the yard, 1" Pink silk rose

INSTRUCTIONS:
Fold rope into a heart shape. Secure with glue. Wrap ribbon around rope. Glue ends. Wrap pearls around rope. Glue ends. Fray ends of rope and separate strands. Glue shells where rope joins. Glue rose to center of shells.

Projects for Kids

Angel Card
by Andrea Gibson

SIZE: 3½" x 3½"
SHELLS: Turitella for body
  Baby Ark (2 for wings, 1 for head)
MATERIALS:
  2 - 3½" squares of White felt
  2½" square of chipboard
  Blue acrylic paint, Brown chalk ink
  Glitter glue for halo, Hot Glue
INSTRUCTIONS:
  Paint chipboard. Let dry. Ink the edges. Glue shells to chipboard. Glue pieces of felt together.
  Glue chipboard to felt. Add a halo.

Flower Note Cards

SIZE: 4" x 4"
SHELLS: Assorted
MATERIALS:
  4" x 8" White cardstock
  3" x 3" chipboard
  Green craft paint, Brown chalk ink
  Twigs
INSTRUCTIONS:
  Paint chipboard Green. Let dry. Fold White cardstock to 4" x 4". Ink the edges.
  Adhere chipboard to front of note card. Glue shells and twigs.

Snake Blackboard
by Linda Valentino

SIZE: 5¾" x 7¾"
SHELLS: 30 small Cerith shells and Snail shells
MATERIALS:
  5¾" x 7¾" blackboard, Paper towel to sponge on paint
  Acrylic paints (Light, Medium, and Dark Green)
  Foam letter stickers, Red foam for tongue, 5mm wiggle eye
INSTRUCTIONS:
  Sponge paints together on blackboard border. Let dry.
  Adhere letters at top. Adhere shells to form a snake shape.
Adhere wiggle eye and Red foam tongue.

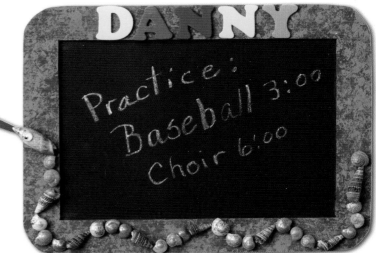

Cut Hemp Cord

Cut hemp cord into 72" long pieces.

Begin with an Overhand Knot

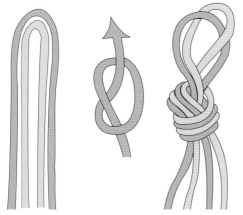

Gather cords and fold them in half.
Follow the diagram to slip the folded end
through a loop made with all the cords.
Pull the knot tight.

Make Half-Hitch Knots

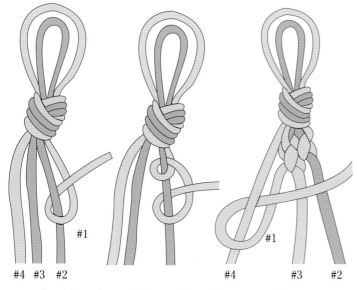

#1

#4 #3 #2

#1

#4   #3   #2

Knot the right cord #1 around cord #2 one time. Knot #1 around #2 a second time. Pull the knot tight.
This completes the first Half-Hitch.
Move to cord #3. Knot #1 around #3 two times. Pull tight.
Move to cord #4. Knot #1 around #4 two times. Pull tight.
If you have more cords, continue in the same manner making knots on a diagonal slant until you reach the end of the row.
Refer to the photo to add seashells that have holes.
Continue knotting until your bracelet is the desired length.

End with an Overhand Knot.

Gather cords. Make another Overhand Knot by slipping the ends through a loop made with all the cords. Pull tight.
Cut off extra cords, leaving only 2 cords to tie to the loop.

Hemp and Seashell Bracelets

Small Bracelet - MATERIALS:
4 Cowrie shells with holes, five ⅜" beads, 2 lengths of 72" hemp cord
INSTRUCTIONS: Make an Overhand Knot. Make 2 rows of diagonal Half-Hitch Knots. Add 1 bead. Make 2 rows of diagonal Half-Hitch Knots. Add a shell. Repeat 4 times or until bracelet is the desired length. On last set do not add shell. Tie an Overhand Knot.

Medium Bracelet - MATERIALS:
20 Cone shells with holes, 3 lengths of 72" hemp cord
INSTRUCTIONS: Make an Overhand Knot. Make 1 row of diagonal Half-Hitch Knots. Add 2 shells. Repeat 9 times or until bracelet is the desired length. Make 1 more row of diagonal Half-Hitch Knots. Tie an Overhand Knot.

Large Bracelet - MATERIALS:
6 Cowrie shells with holes, four ⅜" beads, 5 lengths of 72" hemp cord
INSTRUCTIONS: Make an Overhand Knot. Make 2 rows of diagonal Half-Hitch Knots. Add 2 shells. Make 2 rows of diagonal Half-Hitch Knots. Add 2 beads. Repeat 1 time or until bracelet is the desired length. Make 2 rows of diagonal Half-Hitch Knots. Add 2 shells. Make 2 rows of diagonal Half-Hitch Knots. Tie an Overhand Knot.

Butterfly Door Hanger

SIZE: 6" x 6"
SHELLS:
    Olive shell for body
    4 Scallop shells for wings
MATERIALS:
    Old CD, White paper to cover hole in CD
    6" White paper plate, Decorative edged scissors
    Hole punches ($\frac{1}{8}$", $\frac{1}{16}$"), 12" Blue $\frac{1}{2}$" wide ribbon
    3" Icy Grape 18 gauge wire, Foam letter stickers
    Two 3mm wiggle eyes

INSTRUCTIONS:
    Glue ends of ribbon to the back of the CD.
    Punch holes around the edge of the paper plate to create a pretty pattern. Glue plate to back of CD. Cover hole in center of CD with a White paper circle.
    Glue letters in place. Shape wire into antennae. Position wire and shells. Glue wire first, then glue shells in place. Glue wiggle eyes to Olive shell.

Angel Frame

SIZE: 5" x 7"
SHELLS:
    2 Scallop shells for dresses
MATERIALS:
    5" x 7" paper mache frame
    White gel pen to outline frame
    Acrylic paints: Blue and White (sponged together
      on frame), White for wings, Yellow for star
    Two wooden hearts for each set of wings, $1\frac{1}{8}$", $1\frac{5}{8}$"
    $\frac{7}{8}$" wooden star, Wooden balls for heads ($\frac{1}{2}$", $\frac{3}{4}$")
    2 Yellow 7mm rhinestones, Gold cord
    White chenille stem for arms, Gold tinsel stem for halo
    Doll hair, Fine iridescent glitter for wings
    Marker for face, Red chalk for cheeks
    Paper towels to sponge frame

INSTRUCTIONS:
    Sponge Blue and White paint together on frame. Paint wings White and star Yellow. Let dry.
    Glue wings to body shell. Glue arms. Glue hair on head. Draw face. Chalk cheeks. Glue head in place.
    Glue Gold ribbon bow at neck. Form halo to fit head. Glue star with rhinestone over hands of large angel. Glue rhinestone over hands of small angel. Glue angels to frame.

Bee Happy

SIZE: $2\frac{3}{4}$" x $7\frac{1}{4}$"
SHELLS:
    2 Olive shells for bodies
    4 Jingle shells for wings
MATERIALS:
    $2\frac{3}{4}$" x $7\frac{1}{4}$" wooden plaque
    Foam letter stickers, 4 wiggle eyes 5mm
    Black 22 gauge wire (4", 2")
    15" Blueberry 18 gauge wire
    Acrylic paints (Blue, White, Yellow)
    Black permanent marker (Bold tip for body stripes)
    Paper towel to sponge plaque

INSTRUCTIONS:
    Crumple a paper towel and use it to sponge a mix of Blue and White paint onto plaque.
    Paint Olive shells Yellow. Let dry. Draw body stripes on Olive shells with a bold tip marker. Draw a fine line around the edge of the plaque.
    Attach wire hanger to plaque. Shape wire into antennae. Glue wire to back of Olive shells. Glue letters and shells in place. Glue wiggle eyes to body.

Projects for Kids

My Stuff Box

SIZE: 8" x 11" x 4½" tall

SHELLS:
- 3 Scallop shells for fish bodies
- 3 Ark shells for fish tails
- Assorted small shells
- Starfish

MATERIALS:
- 8" x 11" Blue photo/craft storage box
- Sandpaper for sand, Decorative net
- Acrylic paints (White, Orange, Toffee)
- Alphabet foam stamps, 6mm Wiggle eyes

INSTRUCTIONS:

Paint the Scallop and Ark shells Orange. Let dry. Stamp "My Stuff" on the side of the box with Toffee paint.

Set aside to dry. Tear a piece of sandpaper to fit the length of the lid. Glue in place. Glue small shells, Starfish, and net in place.

Glue Orange shells to form fish. Paint White bubbles. Glue a wiggle eye on each fish. Let dry.

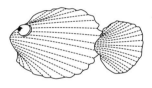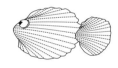

Switch Plates
by Linda Valentino

IZE: 3½" x 6"

SHELLS:
- 2 small Jingle shells for girl shoes
  or Cerith shells for boy shoes
- 2 Scallop shells for dress or 3 small
  clam shells for shirt and shorts
- Cockle shell for boy's hat

MATERIALS:
- 3½" x 6" wooden switch plate
- Acrylic paints (Wisteria for girl,
  Sapphire for boy, Flesh for face,
  Black for eyes, White dot on cheeks)
- Wooden 1¼" circle for face
- Yellow or Orange craft thread for hair
- 22 gauge Black wire for arms and legs
- Black marker for smile and stripes
- Foam letter stickers, Red chalk for cheeks

INSTRUCTIONS:

Paint switch plate and wood circle for face. Let dry. Position shells, head circle, and wires. Glue head and wires to plate first. Adhere shells. Glue hair on head.

Dot eyes with a bit of Black paint. Draw smile. Let dry. Color cheeks with chalk. Add tiny dot of White paint on cheeks.

Draw stripes on shell for boy's shirt.

Projects for Kids

Slow Going

by Andrea Gibson

SIZE: 2¾" x 5"

SHELLS:
Assorted

MATERIALS:
White tag
Green cardstock, Tacky glue
Hero Arts Friendship Alphabet stamps
Sakura Black ink pens (.03, .05), Blue ink
2 Yellow mini brads, 2 Orange paper flowers
Striped ⅝" wide ribbon, Wiggle eye

INSTRUCTIONS:
Ink the edges of the tag. Cut Green paper strips and ink the edges. Adhere to bottom of tag. Cut 2 thin flower stems. Adhere stems and flowers in place. Add brads.

Plan position of snail shell. Doodle a snail. Glue shell and wiggle eye to tag. Stamp letters. Add ribbon.

Cool Fish

SIZE: 4¼" x 6"

SHELLS:
Assorted

MATERIALS:
Hot glue, Black ink
Cardstock (Light Blue, Blue), 7 Blue ½" flat marbles
Alphabet stamps, *Sakura* Black ink pens (.03, .05)

INSTRUCTIONS:
Make a Light Blue card 4¼" x 6". Cut a Blue mat 3½" x 5⅜". Tear one long edge and adhere to card. Stamp message. Glue shells in fish shapes. Draw around the shapes to form fish. Adhere blue marbles.

Penguin

SIZE: 4¼" x 6"

SHELLS:
Coquina shells for body (1 large, 1 small)
2 Mexican Olive shells for arms
Snail shell for head
2 Brown Auger shells for feet

MATERIALS:
Cardstock (Red, White, Black Gingham)
Alphabet stamps, 3 Red square brads
Sakura Black ink pens (.03, .05), Wiggle eyes,

INSTRUCTIONS:
Make a Red card 4¼" x 6". Adhere a Gingham mat 4" x 5¾". Cut a White mat 3½" x 5¼". Ink the edges and stamp message. Attach Red brads. Adhere to card. On Black cardstock, position shells to form penguin. Trace around the edge leaving a ¼" border. Cut out Black penguin shadow.

Adhere to card. Glue shells in place. Glue wiggle eyes to Snail shell.

Decorative "M"
by Andrea Gibson

SIZE: 8" x 9¼"
SHELLS: Assorted small to medium
MATERIALS:
    Precut wood letter (natural or pre-painted White)
    Brown Organza 1¼" wide ribbon
    Tacky glue
INSTRUCTIONS:
    Apply Tacky glue generously to top of letter. Cover letter with shells. Let dry. Staple 2 pieces of ribbon to the back of letter; tie in bow at top for hanging.

Hexagon Box
by Julie McGuffee

SIZE: 7¼" x 7¼" x 3"
SHELLS:
    1 Orange Pecten, 3 Philippine Olive shells
    1 Baby Ark, 2 Turris shells
    1 Babylonia, 3 Venus Clam shells, 1 Bursa Crumena
    1 Rose Cockle, 2 Yellow Banded Snail shells
MATERIALS:
    7¼" hexagon paper mache box
    6" round Ecru crocheted doily, 3" Ecru tassel
    24" Ecru ¼" wide satin ribbon
    24" Ecru 1⅞" wide lace
    Acrylic paint (Buttermilk, Tan)
    Sponge brush, Small sponge
INSTRUCTIONS:
    Paint box with 2 coats of paint. Let dry. Spray box with sealer. Let dry. Glue lace around bottom of box. Glue ribbon around top edge of lace. Glue doily to center of lid. Glue tassel in place.
    Adhere shells on top of doily.

Clay & Shell Projects

by Linda Valentino
BASIC MATERIALS:
Crayola White Model Magic
SHELLS: Assorted small
BASIC INSTRUCTIONS:
    Following instructions on the package to apply Model Magic to project.
    Embed shells. Let dry.

MATERIALS FOR POT:
SIZE: 3" x 3" x 4" tall
    2½" diameter clay pot
    Blue Acrylic paint
    Foam letter stickers
Paint pot Blue. Let dry.

MATERIALS FOR MIRROR:
SIZE: 6½" x 6½"
    6" wood floral ring
    4¾" round mirror
Decorate the ring then glue the mirror to the back.

MATERIALS FOR BOX:
    3¼" x 4¼" box
    2" x 3" Oval mirror
    Blue Acrylic paint
Paint the bottom of the box. Let dry. Glue the mirror to the top of the lid.

Projects for Kids

Gone Fishing Frame
by Andrea Gibson

SIZE: 4¾" x 6¾"

SHELLS:
    Assorted shells

MATERIALS:
    Spanish Moss spray paint (step 1)
    Blue crackle spray paint (step 2)
    Matte spray sealer
    2 yards of jute twine
    Sea net, Sea glass
    Hot glue, 4¾" x 6¾" frame (2¾" x 4¾" window)

INSTRUCTIONS:
    Wrap each side of frame 3 times with twine. Secure in place with glue. Spray paint frame with several heavy coats of Spanish Moss base coat. Let dry for at least 1 hour. Spray several heavy coats of Linen Blue crackle with no drying time between coats.
    Let dry. Spray with matte sealer. Let dry.
    Cut a piece of sea net to fit the corners of the frame. Hot glue in place at net knots to hide glue.
    Adhere sea glass and shells.

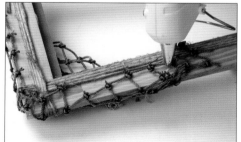

Wonderful Projects for All Ages!

Turtle Magnet
by Nancy Flodine

SIZE: 1" x 2"

SHELLS:
    1" Polished Limpet
    1½" Sugar Starfish

MATERIALS:
    1" Round magnet, Hot glue
    Black permanent marker

INSTRUCTIONS:
    Center and glue Limpet on top of Starfish. Glue magnet on bottom of Starfish. Make small glue dot on each side of face for eyes. Color eyes Black with marker.

Snowman

SIZE: 3¼" x 5"

SHELLS:
    3 White Cockle shells , Black Nerite shell for hat

MATERIALS:
    Mini jumbo craft stick, Mini buttons (2 Black, 1 Orange)
    Two 3mm wiggle eyes, Red ¼" pom pom
    Brown chenille stem (5", 1", 1"), 8" Plaid ½" ribbon for scarf
    White acrylic paint, Red chalk, Gold cord

INSTRUCTIONS:
    Paint craft stick White. Let dry. Glue Cockle shells to stick. Glue Black Nerite to head. Glue eyes, nose, and buttons in place. Rub cheeks with Red chalk. Glue pom pom to tip of hat. Shape arms and hands with Brown stem.
    Glue to back of stick. Wrap ribbon around neck and tie for a scarf. Glue cord to back for hanger.

Flower

SIZE: 2¾" x 2¾"
SHELLS:
　5 Scallop shells for petals, Moon Snail shell for center
　Sea Urchin spine for stem, 2 Turris shells for leaves
INSTRUCTIONS:
　Glue shells to a background to form the flower.

Chick

SIZE: 3½" x 3½"
SHELLS:
　White cockle shell for head, 2 Strawberry Cockle shells - wings
　Scallop shell for body, Tellin shell for beak, 2 Ark shells for feet
MATERIALS:
　Two 7mm wiggle eyes, Yellow feather, Orange acrylic paint
INSTRUCTIONS:
　Paint the Tellin shell Orange. Let dry. Position shells and feather on a background and glue in place.
　Glue eyes and beak in place.

Bunny

SIZE: 2" x 4½"
SHELLS:
　Cockle shell for head, 2 mini Cockle shells - paws
　Scallop shell for body, 3 Auger shells - ears, carrot
MATERIALS:
　Two 7mm wiggle eyes, Two ¼" White pom poms
　⅛" Pink pom pom, Yellow bow, Orange acrylic paint
　1" Green 22 gauge wire
INSTRUCTIONS:
　Paint a small Auger shell Orange for the carrot. Curl the wire and attach for carrot greens. Glue shells to a background forming the shape. Glue eyes, nose, cheeks and bow in place.

Dragonfly

SIZE: 2¾" x 4"
SHELLS:
　Turret shell for body, 4 Ark shells for wings
MATERIALS:
　2 wiggle eyes 5mm , 4" of Blue 18 gauge wire
　Turquoise Pearl acrylic paint
INSTRUCTIONS:
　Paint the Turret shell Turquoise. Let dry. Shape antennae from wire. Glue to back of Turret shell. Glue shells to a background to form the dragonfly. Glue eyes.

Christmas Tree Pin

SIZE: 1½" x 3"
SHELLS:
　3 Scallop shells, Mini Starfish
MATERIALS:
　Mini craft stick, 5mm rhinestones (Red, Yellow, Blue)
　Acrylic paints (Light, Medium and Dark Green, Yellow)
　1" pin back
INSTRUCTIONS:
　Paint the Starfish Yellow. Paint the Scallop shells Light Green on top, Medium Green on middle, and Dark Green on bottom. Let dry.
　Glue the largest Scallop shell to the craft stick, aligning the bottom of the shell with the bottom of the stick. Glue the other Scallop shells and Starfish in place.
　Glue rhinestones to shells. Glue pin back to back of stick.

Flower　　　Chick

Bunny　　　Dragonfly

Remember the joys of
seeing shells embedded in the sand
after a wave washed ashore.

1. Assemble baby. Glue securely into manger shell.
2. Glue yarn bundle at 1 end to create Mary's veil.

3. Glue yarn bundle to Mary's head.
4. Glue trim along front edge of veil.

5. Glue arms to body, points up, opening to the front.
6. Attach cloak. Spread out to cover the back of shell.

Mini-Books with Seashell Covers

A whole new approach to hardback books… use seashells for covers and mulberry paper for pages.

MATERIALS: Handmade mulberry paper, Matching pairs of seashells (Pecten, Irish Flat, Scallop), 1/8" paper punch, Jute cord or raffia, Tape, Drill with 1/16" bit, Wood block

1. Drill holes in seashells. For safety, secure each shell to board with a clamp to hold the shell. Do not hold the shell with your fingers.
2. Trace around shell shape.

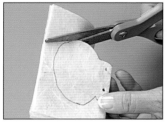

3. Punch holes in the paper and cut out pages.
4. Lace shell covers and pages together.
  Caution: Drill shells outdoors. Do not breathe the dust.

INSTRUCTIONS:
  For each book, place shell on wood block, hold carefully and drill 2 or 4 holes in hinge area of one shell. Mark second shell and drill matching holes.
  Cut mulberry paper into squares slightly larger than shells. Stack sheets, place shell on top, mark holes and trace around shell.
  Remove shell, punch 1/8" holes at marks and cut paper into shell shape.
  Wrap a small piece of tape around end of cord or ribbon to make a point. Thread cord through one shell, paper sheets and other shell.
  Tie cord ends together.

Abalone Nativity Scene
by Nancy Flodine

SIZE: 5" x 6" x 6"

SHELLS:

　　5" Abalone, 4" Irish Flat, 1" Bay Starfish
　　Cerithium Nodulosum center slices (two 4", one 3")
　　1" Strombus Luhuanus for Joseph's body
　　Two ¾" Brown Cones for Joseph's arms
　　Three ³⁄₁₆" Pearl Umboniums for faces
　　Baby Arca (one ¾", two 1", two 1¼")
　　1" White Chula, Two ⅜" White Doves

MATERIALS:

　　3" wire 20 gauge, Brown floral tape
　　Clear acrylic spray, Extra fine Clear acrylic glitter
　　3" White pearl ¼" flowers by the yard
　　3" Brown wired fishnet ribbon #40, Hot glue
　　4" White boucle yarn, Silver lame 2 ply thread

INSTRUCTIONS:

Assemble shells. Glue 1¼" Arca on ¾" Arca for crib. Use 3 Arca shells for Mary's robe. Form Joseph's staff with wire and cover with Brown floral tape.

Driftwood Birds

SIZE: 2" x 11" x 3½" tall

SHELLS:

　　Strombus Canarium for bodies (1 medium, 3 small)
　　Snails for heads (2 medium, 1 small)
　　4 Baby Ark, 2 Cockle, 2 White Scallops for wings
　　4 small Turitella for beaks

MATERIALS:

　　2" x 11" driftwood, Black fine point marker, 2 toothpicks

INSTRUCTIONS:

　　See Diagrams to glue beaks to heads, heads to bodies, and wings to sides. Glue toothpicks to 1 bird. Glue birds to driftwood with Hot glue.

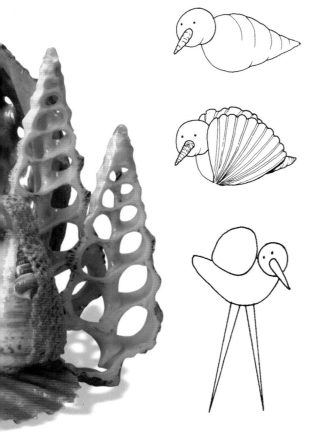

Seaview Birdhouse
by Julie McGuffee

SIZE: 5½" x 6" x 7½"

SHELLS:

　　2 Trochus shells
　　13 Dyed Dove shells
　　　　for star and flowers
　　60 White Chula shells for roof
　　30 Baby Ark shells for roof edge
　　1 small Snail for perch
　　8 Mexican Olive shells for hole
　　6 Turitella shells for star
　　1 Coquina for hole

MATERIALS:

　　Chalet birdhouse
　　Off White spray paint
　　Krylon Stone craft spray paint
　　1" x 1¼" wood rectangle
　　Sisal rope
　　Jute twine
　　½" x 16" sturdy twig
　　Black fine tip permanent marker

INSTRUCTIONS:

Birdhouse:

　　Paint house. Let dry. Cut 8 pieces of rope the same length as the roof. Glue 4 pieces on each side along edges of ridges and at the top. Glue Chula shells to roof and Baby Arks along edges of roof.

Posts:

　　Cut twig into 8 pieces. Glue to edge around base. Starting at the front, glue 1 end of jute to top of post, wrap around each post ending at the post on opposite side of the front. Cut rope to fit between posts and glue along the base.

Sign:

　　Write "Seaview Inn" on wood rectangle. Glue to front. Glue jute around edge and a shell to the top.

Hole:

　　Glue Olive shells around hole, Coquina at the base.

Perch:

　　Wrap jute around perch. Glue in place. Glue small Snail shell to end.

Back of House:

　　Blue Trochus to center and Turitella around Snail shells. Glue small Dove shells in spaces between Turitella shells.

Pillar Candle on a Dish

SIZE: 3" x 6"

SHELLS:
   3 Babylonia shells
   1 Turitella
   2 White Cerithium shells

MATERIALS:
   6" pillar candle
   3" x 10" corrugated cardboard
   Pinking shears
   Raffia

INSTRUCTIONS:
   Cut cardboard with pinking shears 2½" x 10". Wrap around candle and glue in place.
   Wrap raffia around cardboard and tie in a bow.
   Glue shells in center of bow.

Glass Votive Candle Holder

by Linda Valentino

SIZE: 3" x 3" x 3¼" tall

SHELLS:
   35 Jingle shells

MATERIALS:
   3" glass votive candle holder
   Sculpey Translucent modeling compound
   White votive candle
   Fine Iridescent glitter

INSTRUCTIONS:
   Following the package instructions, cover a glass candle holder with modeling compound. Embed shells. Bake for 15 minutes in a 275 degree oven.

   Optional: Use translucent polymer clay in place of modeling compound. Bake as recommended on the package.

Supplier - Most craft and variety stores carry an excellent assortment of supplies. If you need something special, ask your local store to contact the following companies:

SEASHELLS - U.S. Shell
ADHESIVES - Beacon, Eclectic Products

MANY THANKS to my associates for their cheerful help and wonderful ideas!
Kathy Mason • Patty Williams
Donna Kinsey • Kristy Krouse
David & Donna Thomason

Shell Doll

by Julie McGuffee

SIZE: 4½" x 4½" x 4" tall

SHELLS:
   3 Baking Dish shells for dress, 1 Pink Pecten for apron
   1 White Pecten for hat, 2 Turitella shells for arms

MATERIALS:
   1" wood ball knob, 9" of Pink satin ¼" ribbon
   4x9mm teardrop pearl charm, Beige curly wool hair
   Pink cosmetic blush, 4" of thin wire
   Black fine tip permanent marker

INSTRUCTIONS:
   Skirt: Glue Baking Dish shells as shown in diagram. Adhere Pink Pecten for apron.

   Head: Glue head in place.

   Face: Rub blush on face. Dot eyes with a marker. Glue hair. Glue Pink Pecten to back of head for hat.

   Arms: Glue Turitella shells.

   Bow: Make a ribbon bow and secure with wire. Attach pearl with wire. Glue bow to front.

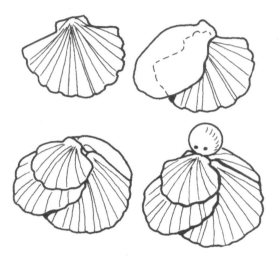

Angel Pin

SIZE: 1½" x 2"

SHELLS:
   3 Baby Ark shells, l slightly larger for dress, 2 small Snail shells for hands

MATERIALS:
   1" pin back, ½" wood bead, Small piece of Blonde curly hair
   Gold ring, ¼" Pink porcelain rose, 2 White 4mm x 9mm teardrop pearls
   Black fine tip permanent marker, Waxed paper

INSTRUCTIONS:
   Arrange Baby Ark shells flat side down on waxed paper. Glue wood bead where shells meet. Glue Snail shells on sides of bead. Adhere rose and pearls to front. Glue hair to head. Glue Gold ring to shells behind head. Let dry.

   Remove from waxed paper. Adhere pin back. Dot eyes with marker.

Hat Pin

SIZE: 2" x 2"

SHELLS:
   Craft shells (5 tiny, 1 small) , 4 tiny Coquina shells, 7 Dyed Dove shells

MATERIALS:
   2" straw hat, 4" Ivory ½" wide ruffled lace, 12" Ivory ¼" wide satin ribbon
   4" White 3mm pearls by the yard, 1" wood circle, Pin back

INSTRUCTIONS:
   Glue lace around hat brim. Glue ribbon around hat crown and pearls on top of ribbon. Tie bow with remaining ribbon and glue to hat brim.

   Glue wood circle over opening at back of hat. Glue pin back to wood circle.

Heart Box

SIZE: 3" x 3" x 1½" tall

SHELLS:
   Small Pink Craft shells, 1 Pearlized Turbo, 5 Dove shells

MATERIALS:
   3" heart box, 12" Off White ½" wide ruffled lace
   12" of Lavender ⅛" wide satin ribbon
   12" of White 4mm pearls by the yard
   Buttermilk acrylic paint

INSTRUCTIONS:
   Paint box. Let dry. Glue lace, ribbon, and pearls around edge of lid. Starting at the outside edge, glue Pink shells to lid with flat sides down. Glue Turbo to top center. Arrange and glue 5 Pink shells, flat side up, around Turbo; glue a pearl inside each. Glue Dove shells between craft shells.

Heart Pin

SIZE: 2" x 2¼"

SHELLS:
   12 small Coquina shells, 7 Dyed Trochus

MATERIALS:
   1" pin back, 2 wood hearts 1½"
   5" Off White ruffled ½" wide lace
   5" Blue ⅛" wide ribbon, ¼" Pink porcelain rose
   5" Off White 3mm pearls by the yard
   Buttermilk acrylic paint

INSTRUCTIONS:
   Paint hearts. Let dry. Glue lace on top of one heart around the edge. Glue second heart over first heart, sandwiching the lace. Glue pearls around edge of top heart.

   Glue shells and ribbon bow in place. Glue pin back in place.

Mule Ear Abalone

Arrowhead Sand Dollar

Calico Pecten Orange

Calico Pecten Pink

Irish Flat

Abalone

Coquina Purple

Astrea Calcar

Pink Scallop

White Pearlized Turbo

Pitar Rosea

Gar Scales

Bear's Paw

Abalone Chips

Brown Auger

Brown Cone

Cone Cut

Bursa Rana

Cerithium Vertagus Center Slice

Green Turbo Center Slice

Ring Top Cowrie

Green Mexican Limpet

Cancelaria Undulata

Sundial

Pearlized Top

Cerithium Vertagus

White Cockle

Tree Snail

Round Slice

Bay Starfish

Keyhole Sand Dollar

Sunrise Tellina

Small White Cockle

White Sun/Moon

Cowrie - Purple Diagonal Cut

Cowrie Sliced

Sea Biscuit

Dogwood Clams

Mitra Ru-gosum

Lion's Paw

Sugar Starfish

Keyhole Limpet

Pecten Phallium

Irish Deep

Pecten Albican

Land Snail

Fiber Conch

White Baby Arca

Crown Conch

White Auger

Sea Urchin Spine

Fusinus Center Slice

Philippine Yellow Cockle

Pearlized Umboniums

Beige Nassa

Kitten's Paw

Polished Limpet

Chione - Purple

Lophiotoma Center Slice

Strombus Luhuanus Center & Diagonal Slice

Turitella Terebra

Purple Drupa

Purple Drupa Center Slice

Pecten Noblis

Philippine Dove

Purple Drupa Edge Slices

White Nassa

White Chula & Center Slice

Cerithium Nodulosum Center Slice

Cheena Clam

Brown Chula

Brown Chula Center Slice

UPC code

ISBN 157421330-X

0 023863 034531

9 781574 213300

50899

Design Originals

www.d-originals.com

2425 CULLEN STREET
FORT WORTH, TX 76107